THE IDENTIFICATION, BEHAVIOUR AND NATURAL HISTORY OF THE

SHARKS

OF FLORIDA, THE BAHAMAS, THE CARIBBEAN, THE GULF OF MEXICO

IN DEPTH
ADVENTURE GUIDES

THE IDENTIFICATION, BEHAVIOUR AND NATURAL HISTORY OF THE

SHARKS

OF FLORIDA, THE BAHAMAS, THE CARIBBEAN, THE GULF OF MEXICO

Jeremy Stafford-Deitsch

TRIDENT
PRESS

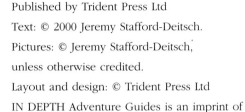

Published by Trident Press Ltd

Text: © 2000 Jeremy Stafford-Deitsch.

Pictures: © Jeremy Stafford-Deitsch,
unless otherwise credited.

Layout and design: © Trident Press Ltd

IN DEPTH Adventure Guides is an imprint of
Trident Press.

Series Editor: Peter Vine

Illustrations: Ian Fergusson

Typesetting and layout: Justin King

British Library Cataloguing in Publication Data.
A CIP Catalogue record for this book is available
from the British Library.

ISBN: 1-900724-44-8 HARDBACK
ISBN: 1-900724-45-6 PAPERBACK

Trident Press Ltd
175 Piccadilly,
London, W1V 9DB
United Kingdom
Tel: 020 7491 8770
Fax: 020 7491 8664
Email: admin@tridentpress.ie
Internet: www.tridentpress.com

IN DEPTH Adventure Guides are small, affordable guide books packed with 'must-have' information for active people pursuing a wide range of outdoor activities. The imprint title, IN DEPTH, alludes firstly to the fact that many of the books in the series will deal with underwater subjects – such as guides to sharks of different regions; and secondly to the in depth nature of the information within these small guides – all of which are written by experts in their respective fields.

IN DEPTH Adventure Guides aim to provide accurate information, based on first-hand descriptions of wildlife, natural environments and related subjects.

CONTENTS

WE ARE IN A STATE OF TRANSITION. Thirty years ago divers were advised that the best thing to do if you saw a shark was to get out of the water. Nowadays the majority of divers hope to dive with sharks just as a tourist on an African safari hopes to see big cats.

Biologists who have spent many hours watching sharks in their natural habitat have begun to observe a variety of heretofore unsuspected behaviour patterns both within and between species. The old clichés – that a shark is a shark is a shark, that they are no more than primitive eating machines, that the only good shark is a dead shark, that they have not evolved in hundreds of millions of years – are crumbling as glimpses into their considerable sophistication force a re-evaluation. But it is only a few minutes before midnight: shark species the world over are threatened with extinction.

Dive operators are now finding themselves in the novel position of being expected to offer shark dives, in which the local sharks are fed so as to bring them in close. This is something of a mixed blessing: divers who can interact with sharks underwater, who can appreciate first-hand their splendour, can and must contribute to conservation initiatives. The downside to shark feeding, it has been argued, is that regular feeds disrupt the fragile ecology of the habitats in which they occur. Furthermore, it has been suggested that the sharks in question lose their natural timidity towards humans: the risk of attack therefore, presumably, increases. And it is certainly true that, very, very occasionally, someone – usually the feeder – does get bitten.

[opposite]
The spectacular Chumsicke Feed at Walker's Cay, the Bahamas, has a flawless safety record.

[opposite]
Encounters with the whale shark *Rhincodon typus* are rare but possible throughout this region.

As an underwater photographer I know full well that most sharks need to be attracted by food if they are to be photographed. And it seems to me that responsible shark-feeding operations have a crucial role to play in educating the public about the reality of sharks. The risks are small, the rewards tremendous.

There are few non-specialist books dealing with shark identification. Even fewer cater specifically for divers. Scientists often rely on a host of esoteric details, such as tooth number and shape, vertebral count, proportion of fin height to total body length, to separate similar-looking species, but such details usually require a carcass. Most of the species discussed herein can be readily identified underwater due to certain prominent features. A few can not: for example a free-swimming Galapagos shark and Caribbean reef shark are difficult to distinguish.

The aim of this guide is to provide a sketch of the natural history and behaviour of sharks in general and then to facilitate the identification of sharks that a diver in the warm waters from Florida to the northern shore of South America is more likely to encounter. None of the species described in this guide is confined to this artificially-created region and some are ocean wanderers that occur worldwide.

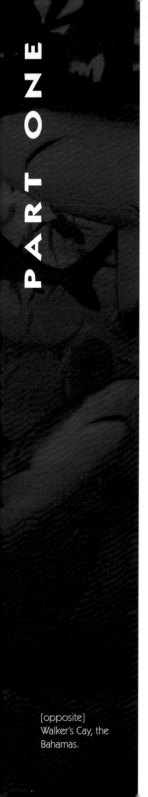

PART ONE

SHARKS AND THEIR RELATIVES

Sharks belong to an ancient and extraordinary side-branch of evolution that can be traced back some 400 million years in the fossil record. The group includes two other remarkable classes of fish: rays and chimaeras. (The term skate refers to members of the same group as the rays.) Rays are familiar enough to divers. Their more impressive members include the eagle ray *Aetobatus narinari* and the manta ray *Manta birostris*. Pioneering research on the eagle ray in Bimini, the Bahamas, has shown that this is a highly social animal equipped with a dozen or more behaviour patterns. Some patterns, such as 'dipping', are performed by one animal to another. Furthermore, the foraging, aggregating and socializing activities of the Bimini eagle rays appear to be geared to specific phases of the tidal cycle. The rays disperse at high tide and forage far afield as the tide begins to fall. At low tide they aggregate in specific core areas. Several of the larger predatory sharks include rays in their diet. Given the tendency of such sharks to move into shallow water on a *rising* tide, it is interesting to ponder whether the movements of the eagle rays are, at least to some degree, designed to minimize confrontation with such sharks.

Chimaeras are small, mostly deep-water creatures that are grouped with sharks and rays as much by default as by design. They are rarely seen by divers.

The vast majority of the world's fishes, some 95 per cent, have a bony skeleton and are collectively termed bony fishes. The skeleton of sharks, rays and chimaeras is composed of cartilage and they are referred to as cartilaginous fishes. In fact cartilaginous fishes differ

[opposite]
Walker's Cay, the
Bahamas.

Larger predatory sharks feed on a variety of rays. This eagle ray *Aetobatus narinari* in Bimini, the Bahamas, had a lucky escape.

from bony fishes in a wide variety of ways including their reproductive, developmental and excretory methods, digestive system, skeletal structure (for instance, ribs which, when present, do not protect the internal organs), sensory mechanisms, the composition of the skin and the lack of a swim bladder. Furthermore, sharks and rays have numerous gill openings on each side of the head or body (normally five), although chimaeras, like bony fishes, have only one. Indeed, so different are the cartilaginous fishes from the bony fishes in so many fundamental details that some experts wonder whether the former should be called fishes at all.

The southern stingray *Dasyatis americana* is a commonly seen ray throughout the region. In certain areas it has become a tourist attraction in its own right.

GENERALIZED SHARK

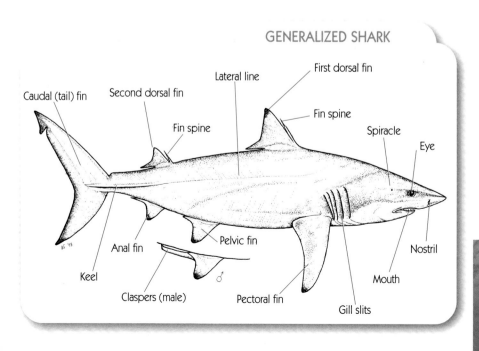

Caudal (tail) fin

Second dorsal fin

Lateral line

First dorsal fin

Fin spine

Fin spine

Spiracle

Eye

Anal fin

Pelvic fin

Keel

Nostril

Claspers (male)

Pectoral fin

Mouth

Gill slits

Distinguishing a shark from a ray is usually simple enough. Most sharks are basically cylinder-shaped and free-swimming, while rays are flattened and the majority are typically encountered on the seabed or swimming sluggishly just above it. However, there are members of both groups that are often mistaken by the lay person: sharks that are erroneously called rays and *vice versa*. Angel sharks (of which one species occurs in our region), are flattened like rays and lie in ambush on the bottom. Guitarfishes, members of the ray group, are occasionally seen by divers and are all too often erroneously called guitarsharks. In fact, a general method of distinguishing sharks from rays is to search for the gill openings: if they are on the side of the body then one is looking at a shark; if they are on the underside, it is a ray.

Furthermore, confusion can arise between sawfishes and sawsharks, both of which have an elongated, tooth-lined snout. There is a species of sawshark that occurs from Florida to Cuba and the Bahamas, but it lives far beyond scuba-diving depth.

As more and more deep-water sharks are recorded from around the world so the species number gradually rises. At present there are over 400 known species. Many of these sharks are relatively small (less than 1 metre in length) and occur at depths beyond the reach of divers. There are also, at these greater depths, impressive shark predators. An example is the bignose shark *Carcharhinus altimus* which occurs in our region and typically cruises just over the substrate in water of a hundred or more metres in depth.

HABITAT PREFERENCES

Some species of shark are fairly habitat-specific: for example, the bull shark *Carcharhinus leucas* tends to occur in shallow, inshore habitats including sea-grass beds and estuaries. Here it typically cruises just off the bottom. The bulk of the bull shark might suggest that it is a sluggish animal. However, its bulbous dimensions presumably displace water efficiently. It is surprisingly agile and capable of accelerating to and maintaining impressive speed. A bull shark has been observed charging straight at a tarpon which it slammed into from side on and carried away, the shark's trajectory and momentum being unaffected.

At Walker's Cay in the Bahamas, bull sharks are common, during the winter months, immediately off the island, but only occasionally encountered on the coral reefs beyond the sea-grass beds. Here, it is the Caribbean

The bignose shark *Carcharhinus altimus* is a large and impressive requiem shark that normally cruises below the reaches of scuba divers. This one was caught and released by a fisherman.

Bull sharks *Carcharhinus leucas* are large and powerful hunters of inshore tropical waters that often travel in pairs.

reef shark *Carcharhinus perezi* that is the dominant shark predator. While the common name suggests that this shark is virtually confined to coral reefs, the truth is rather that this is where divers tend to see the species because divers dive coral reefs. Tagging studies have shown that Caribbean reef sharks venture far offshore into blue water, where they are presumably feeding on pelagic tuna.

The Caribbean reef shark can occur in impressive numbers on healthy reefs and is the species commonly fed by dive operators throughout this region. An example of a superb coral reef supporting 30 or more hefty Caribbean reef sharks occurs some 15 kilometres south of the western tip of New Providence Island in the Bahamas. The local operators dive this reef for its own sake and also feed the sharks for the spectacle of divers. Given the richness of these reefs, the impressive numbers of sharks that they can support, and the considerable revenue derived from divers visiting such reefs to dive with the sharks, it is a wonder that local governments have not instantly granted such locations protected status against fishermen. Even in the crudest economic terms protection is only common sense. A fisherman might make a handful of dollars from the carcass (or more specifically, the fins) of a shark. On the other hand, the shark, having been incorporated into the local tourist economy as a star attraction, will be worth, annually, tens of thousands of dollars.

Other habitats can also be crucial for a given shark species. The lemon shark *Negaprion brevirostris* tends to give birth in sheltered, mangrove-fringed lagoons. Juvenile lemon sharks require this food-rich, inter-tidal ecosystem for their development. Destruction of the mangroves in a region can be expected to decimate the local lemon shark population.

The Caribbean reef shark is an apex predator of western Atlantic coral reefs. It requires healthy reefs in order to flourish.

The two most formidable shark species likely to be encountered by a diver in this region – the tiger shark *Galeocerdo cuvier* and the great hammerhead *Sphyrna mokarran* – are predators with a broad diet; neither appears to be much concerned by the subtleties of habitat. While either can be encountered in the shallowest water to the deepest, there is evidence that, at least in this part of the world, tiger sharks tend to come in to shallow water at night and move to deep water during the day.

SEASONALITY AND TEMPERATURE

The presence of a specific shark species in a given location can vary seasonally. Many of the larger species of coastal shark such as the sandbar *Carcharhinus plumbeus*, the dusky *C. obscurus* and the tiger shark *Galeocerdo cuvier* migrate northwards along the eastern seaboard of the United States during the summer months, returning to the warmer Gulf of Mexico/Caribbean 'pool' as the climate cools. Conversely, during the spring plankton bloom, the basking shark *Cetorhinus maximus*, a plankton-feeder that may reach over 10 metres in length, will migrate south from the cold waters of the northwestern Atlantic as far as the east coast of Florida.

Most sharks (including those discussed above) are cold-blooded: the body temperature is virtually the same

Lemon shark *Negaprion brevirostris* pups require mangrove-fringed lagoons for their safety and food supply.

as that of the external environment. This means that they are able to survive within a fairly limited temperature range. The blue shark *Prionace glauca* is an open water species that prefers an ambient temperature range from about 7 to 16°C. It does however occur in the tropics but is found in deeper, colder water.

Several species of shark are able to maintain a body temperature higher than that of their surroundings. Members of the mackerel shark group – including the great white shark *Carcharodon carcharias* and the shortfin mako *Isurus oxyrinchus* – can hold a body temperature of 14°C above that of the environment. This is achieved by what is termed a counter-current exchange system. Venous blood is warmed by muscular activity. The blood vessels that contain this blood run alongside the cooler arterial blood travelling into the animal from the gills. This allows the heat of the former to warm the latter. The temperature at which the vital organs are maintained enables them to function more efficiently.

The shortfin mako occurs worldwide in temperate and tropical waters and, at least in the North Atlantic, prefers water temperature in the range from 17 to 22°C. Larger individuals tend to occur in the region covered in this book. A mako tagged with a sonic transmitter off Cape Canaveral, Florida, in 1978, tended to swim in water within the 18 to 20°C temperature range at several hundred metres depth. Hence the shortfin mako is rarely seen by divers in our region. The great white shark is recorded from Florida, the northern Gulf of Mexico, the Virgin Islands, the Bahamas, Florida and Cuba. It is, however, sufficiently rare not to be included in Part Two of this book.

SWIMMING AND RESPIRING

Unlike bony fishes, sharks lack a swim bladder – a gas-filled sack for buoyancy control. This has given rise to the myth that all sharks, being heavier than water, must swim or sink. A sealed gas-filled bladder is not a good idea for an animal that moves rapidly up and down in the water column (as all divers know). In fact, most sharks have a large liver in which they store oils that are lighter than sea water and this is an efficient means of buoyancy control, independent of depth. Furthermore, the fin and head shape of a free-swimming shark naturally impart upward lift to minimize the effort needed to swim without sinking. Some species of shark intentionally swallow air to make themselves lighter. The sand tiger shark *Carcharias taurus* has perfected this technique and uses its stomach as a buoyancy chamber. This allows the animal to hover. One diver told me of a scalloped hammerhead shark *Sphyrna lewini* that swam up towards him from the depths, belching air as it approached. And one occasionally sees tiger sharks apparently floating and dozing on the surface – it is hard to imagine that they have not gulped a few mouthfuls of air to stay there.

Without such tricks, the tendency of a shark to sink is considerable. I remember once trying to lift a dead 3 metre great hammerhead *Sphyrrna mokarran* off the bottom in the Bahamas. It required a buoyancy compensator filled with air and a great deal of finning.

It is commonly thought that a shark must swim constantly to pass water over the gills, in order to avoid suffocating. The water flowing through the gills meets blood vessels carrying deoxygenated blood *towards* the water, which considerably increases the efficiency of oxygen extraction. In fact, many species are perfectly capable of lying on the bottom and pumping water over the gills. It may simply be that in some species it requires more energy to pump water through the gills than it does to cruise. Furthermore, the likelihood of encountering a potential prey item is greatly enhanced when an animal is moving.

The obvious example of a shark in our region that spends considerable periods of time lying on the substrate is the nurse shark *Ginglymostoma cirratum*. The nostrils of a shark function for smell and do not connect to the gills. Free-swimming sharks take in water that passes to the gills through the mouth. Most sharks have the mouth located on the underside of the head (an adaptation derived from the distant past when their ancestors lived on and ate items from the sea floor). One of the problems

[opposite]
Large (3 metres or more) shortfin makos *Isurus oxyrinchus* prefer warmer waters and are common offshore sharks in this region. The speed, vigour and spectacular fighting abilities of this species has made it the target of sports fishermen. The quality of its meat means that commercial fishermen have decimated its populations.

of lying on a sandy substrate is that sand particles can be taken in by the mouth and interfere with the delicate blood vessels of the gills. For this reason sharks that are adapted to spending a great deal of time on the seabed, such as the nurse shark (and likewise rays), usually have an alternative opening for taking in water: an orifice behind each eye called the spiracle, which minimizes the intake of sand. The spiracle is also found in free-swimming sharks, suggesting it has further, yet to be discovered, functions. In some rays, the developing embryos receive nutrients via threads that pass from the mother's uterus, through the embryo's spiracles, into its gut.

SENSORY MECHANISMS

Sharks have a range of extremely sophisticated sensory mechanisms for locating prey. The most long-range detects vibrations passing through the water, in other words, underwater sound. Scientists have shown that sharks are attracted over distances of several kilometres to artificial low frequency sound pulses that correspond to sounds produced by a struggling fish. Not only do sharks have ears (though without conspicuous external parts), but they also have a pressure-sensitive lateral line extending down each side of the body which detects water-borne vibrations. And it is not just sound that the lateral line detects: disturbances in the water will, at close range, bounce off objects. This means that a shark can detect such objects. As it swims, the waves generated by the shark's own body will interact with the water that envelops it. This allows the shark to detect currents and water movement.

The very large olfactory centres in the brain of a shark attest to the importance of smell for locating food. Indeed, experiments in aquaria show that sharks can smell the most minute concentrations of the appropriate items. The Atlantic lemon shark *Negaprion brevirostris* can detect one part of tuna extract in 25 million parts of water, while it is claimed that the Indo-Pacific grey reef shark *Carcharhinus amblyrhynchos* is able to detect one part of tuna extract in an almost unbelievable 10 billion parts of water. Little wonder that sharks are sometimes referred to as swimming noses.

The eyes of sharks are designed to see well in low light situations and many species are capable of colour

The eye, nostril and sensory pores of the great white shark *Carcharodon carcharias* are visible in this photograph. Note also the retracted teeth of the upper jaw and also replacement teeth in the lower: sharks constantly grow new teeth to replace old ones and get through thousands in a lifetime.

vision. The presence of a tapetum layer in the eye of many species allows for good nocturnal vision as well: the limited available light that enters the eye is reflected back off the tapetum and is therefore amplified. It is of little comfort for a diver, who presumes herself to be safely concealed in the inky blackness of a night dive, to know that any nearby shark can doubtless sense her location by its lateral line and see her with its night vision!

Many sharks, such as the requiem sharks (members of the genus *Carcharhinus* which includes, for example, the Caribbean reef shark), have a unique eyelid termed the nictitating membrane, that closes to protect the eye in a 'blink response' when the snout touches something, or when the shark is feeding. Others, such as the great white, lack this adaptation and actually roll the eye round into its socket for protection.

The snout of a shark is peppered with small jelly-filled pores called the ampullae of Lorenzini. These detect the small electrical fields produced by living creatures. An animal such as a flatfish that buries itself in the sand will, therefore, not be concealed from a hunting shark that passes close by. It has also been suggested that sharks can use this sense to detect the earth's own magnetic field and hence navigate.

REPRODUCTION AND DEVELOPMENT

An objective consideration of the sensory mechanisms of a shark suggests that one is dealing with an immensely sophisticated animal – certainly not the primitive eating machine that the popular press would have us believe. This view is more than confirmed when one considers the reproductive processes. Bony fishes produce massive numbers of eggs and sperm, and fertilization occurs outside the body. When one compares the quantity of raw materials used with the number of mature survivors of the next generation, this can be seen to be a very inefficient process, although with one vital advantage: while populations of bony fishes can fluctuate considerably, the ability to 'saturate' the environment with developing young means that they can bounce back from local disasters. Sharks (and the other cartilaginous fishes) have employed a different strategy for hundreds of millions of years, a strategy that has proved successful up until the last few decades. Fertilization is internal. Indeed, a mature male shark can easily be identified underwater by the presence of claspers – intromittent organs – extending backwards from between the pelvic fins. Furthermore, female sharks are often bulkier than males of the same species and can take on remarkable proportions.

Shark courtship has occasionally been witnessed in the wild. The female presumably produces pheromones (scent signals) to attract the male: divers occasionally see a female shark with several male sharks following closely behind which have been attracted by a scent signal as a precursor to mating. In many species the male will take hold of the female with its teeth during mating and the gashes and scars from such encounters are commonplace on mature female sharks. (In some species the female has thicker skin than the male.)

Once fertilization has occurred there are three basic methods of development. The most primitive is termed ovipary: the developing young is expelled from the mother's body in a yolk-filled egg case. The egg case

[opposite top]
The claspers extending back from the pelvic fins of the male blacktip shark *Carcharhinus limbatus* distinguish it from the female.

[opposite bottom]
Female sharks, such as this female bull shark, can, even when not pregnant, put on considerable bulk compared to conspecific males.

usually has tendrils of some sort to attach it to the seabed or to seaweed. Alternatively, it may be corkscrew-shaped permitting it to be anchored in the sand or wedged in a gully. Once the pup has exhausted its supply of yolk it must struggle out of the egg case and face the risks of the open sea. None of the sharks discussed in Part Two is oviparous.

The most common developmental method of sharks is termed ovovivipary (also termed aplacental vivipary). In this method the pup develops within the relative safety of the mother's uterus. Each pup has a yolk sac attached to it for nourishment. In some species, unfertilized eggs are also devoured by the young, while in others the smaller pups are devoured by the larger – a technique termed intra-uterine cannibalism. The shortfin mako and the sandtiger shark *Carcharias taurus* are ovoviviparous intra-uterine cannibals.

The most advanced method of development in sharks is termed vivipary (also termed placental vivipary). This process parallels that of mammals in that a placental connection is established between the mother and the pup – although sharks invented this method long before mammals were a twinkle in Mother Nature's eye. The majority of the sharks described in Part Two are viviparous. All the requiem sharks are viviparous, with the sole exception of the tiger shark which is ovoviviparous (though it does not appear to practice intra-uterine cannibalism). The hammerheads (family Sphyrnidae), which are thought to have evolved from the requiem sharks only a few tens of millions of years ago, are also viviparous.

[opposite top]
The suction organs on the flattened head of these suckerfishes *Echeneis naucrates* is clearly visible.

[opposite bottom]
This Caribbean reef shark off Andros Island appears to have a gigantic and unidentified leech-like ectoparasite attached to its first dorsal fin.

It is not unusual to see suckerfishes either attached to, or swimming next to, a shark. There are several species, of which the sharksucker *Echeneis naucrates* is the most commonly seen on inshore shark species. The upper surface of the head of the suckerfish is flattened into a suction disc that can be used to attach the animal to the host. The suckerfish then receives a free ride. Some species will attach to a variety of hosts while others are fairly specific in their requirements. If a suckerfish tries to attach to a sensitive part of a shark – such as its snout or lateral line – the shark will twist and writhe to try to free itself of the pest.

Jacks – both adults and juveniles – will often mass around a particular shark, perhaps for protection, perhaps to use its hide to rub themselves free of parasites. Sometimes such a fish-engulfed shark has been observed to swim over to another shark and then go berserk – snapping its jaws and swerving around – until the unwanted jacks leave it and surround the other, more docile shark!

Open-water sharks are often accompanied by another species of jack, the pilotfish *Naucrates ductor*. The myth that pilotfishes guide their host to prey is erroneously derived from the fact that pilotfishes (especially juveniles) often ride the pressure wave immediately in front of the snout of their host. Interestingly enough, while juvenile pilotfishes will accompany a variety of open-water sharks, the adults very much prefer to accompany the oceanic whitetip shark *Carcharhinus longimanus*.

CONSERVATION

Sharks produce only a few pups at a time – miniature versions of the adult. Each pup has a reasonable chance of surviving into adulthood provided that the challenges under which the species established itself remain constant. An advantage of this process is that, once established, the animal in question can exist at the carrying capacity of the habitat – the maximum number of individuals that the habitat can sustain. A crucial disadvantage – as we are about to see – is that if the pressures facing the animal in question increase dramatically, then it may not be able to bounce back and re-establish itself. For example, it has been calculated that if more than 5 per cent of a population of sharks is removed annually from a given area, the entire population will soon collapse. Work has been done on the lemon shark that vividly demonstrates this vulnerability. It can take a female lemon shark 15 years to reach sexual maturity. Pregnancy lasts a year and the female will not mate again for another year after the birth of her pups. Typically 8 – 12 pups are born each alternate year. The mortality of these pups in the first year is about 50 per cent. Only one to three pups are likely to survive into the third year – and there are another 12 years to go before the female reaches sexual maturity (the male can mature sooner). If the number of sharks being killed increases rapidly, then the ability of surviving sharks to fill the gap collapses. In the words of Dr Samuel Gruber, who has studied the lemon sharks of Bimini for many decades, 'sharks barely replace themselves.'

Traditionally, sharks faced predation from relatively few sources. The first is from larger sharks. Bull and tiger sharks

certainly feed on smaller sharks. The shark feed at Walker's
Cay in the Bahamas is usually populated by Caribbean reef
sharks, nurse sharks and blacktips *Carcharhinus limbatus.*
However, the dive masters can always tell when something
larger is lurking in the background because these sharks
become noticeably more nervous and skittish. Another
predatory threat to sharks is the killer whale. But in the
last few decades an enormous new threat has appeared.
The crisis facing the world's shark populations is caused
by unregulated commercial fishing. It is estimated that
well over 100 million sharks are caught annually by
commercial fishing fleets and, as we have seen, sharks
simply do not have the reproductive capacity to survive
this. Furthermore, many species are sexually segregated
for much of their life, which means that catching all the
sharks in a given area can eradicate one sex.

Some sharks are targeted for their flesh – for example, the shortfin mako tastes as good as any quality fish – others are hunted for their liver oil or skin. Sharks are even being caught to provide cartilage pills for pseudo-scientific miracle cures for cancer that do not work. Sports fishermen like to demonstrate their heroism by catching sharks. There is a considerable trophy industry for shark parts: jaws to be hung in vulgar display and teeth to be worn in jewellery. Huge numbers of sharks die because they are accidentally caught on commercial long-lines, which are intended for other creatures such as swordfishes. However, the greatest threat facing the world's sharks is the international trade in shark fins. The fins are used to produce shark fin soup, an oriental delicacy for which supply has never matched the huge demand. With the vast increase in oriental restaurants the world over, the demand has now reached insatiable proportions. A fisherman can catch a shark, slice off the valuable fins and throw the body – dead or alive – back into the sea. The fins are light and easily stored in some out of the way part of the boat while the hold is filled with more commercially valuable fishes such as tuna and swordfish. Dealers in the Far East who used to trade in animal parts such as rhino horn, elephant ivory, tiger penises and bear gall bladders, have side-stepped the international outcry that such imports have occasioned and switched instead to the decimation of sharks for their fins. Given the basic disinterest – hostility even – with which sharks are viewed by the general public, conservation initiatives have been slow and governmental action even slower.

[opposite]
Feeding sharks will tend to establish a dominance hierarchy whereby larger individuals will feed before smaller individuals. While feeding massive bull sharks fish scraps at Walker's Cay, this considerably smaller, but more agile blacktip sped in and for several minutes darted between the bull sharks to snatch fish scraps. Whenever a bull shark swam towards it, the blacktip executed frantic evasive action.

For several years a Commercial Shark Fishery Observer Program has been in operation in the waters of the southeastern United States. The Gulf and South Atlantic Fisheries Development Foundation, in association with ichthyologists of the Florida Museum of Natural History, have placed observers on co-operating commercial boats to monitor shark catch.

Alarmingly, it is now estimated that 85 per cent of the large coastal shark species of the southeastern United States has been killed. On 30 June 1999, attempts by the National Marine Fisheries Service to make commercial shark quotas more stringent were overturned by court order. It was a victory for commercial fishermen as they were again permitted to catch some 14 species of shark desperately in need of protection – first and foremost the dusky shark *Carcharhinus obscurus*.

In November 1999, the United States Congress voted unanimously to ban shark finning in all U.S. waters. The resolution (House Concurrent Resolution #189) does not have the force of law but at the time of writing, moves are afoot to pass the appropriate bill. It remains to be seen whether the National Marine Fisheries Service will manage to introduce sufficiently stringent commercial fishing controls for shark populations in the region to recover. Given the migratory nature of many shark species as well as commercial fishing fleets, anything less than enforced international prohibitions are likely to be ineffective.

Scuba divers who have the opportunity to dive with sharks and to see these magnificent predators in their natural state have a moral obligation to speak up for and support their protection.

If you are interested in more detailed information on the identification, biology and conservation of sharks, two recommended web-sites are those of the Florida Museum of Natural History (www.flmnh.ufl.edu/fish) and The Shark Trust (www.sharktrust.org).

DIVING WITH SHARKS

Diving with sharks is, in the vast majority of cases, safe. This is because even those sharks that are capable of devouring a human being do not have the slightest idea what a diver is. They may be curious, but it is a curiosity typically tinged with caution: more often than not, sharks view divers with trepidation and keep their distance.

There have only been a few occasions in hundreds of my own shark encounters where I have considered myself to be in any danger, and the wisdom of hindsight has normally made it clear why. At the end of this chapter I offer advice derived from my own experiences.

DANGER AND DIET

Different species of shark eat different things – for example, a species such as the nurse shark, that specializes in eating crustaceans and molluscs, has teeth designed for crushing through their shells. Such an animal is hardly likely to try to devour a human being, but will bite defensively if molested or threatened. The bite of a nurse shark is immensely powerful and they do not always let go; a molested nurse shark can remain clamped on to its molester even after having been dispatched.

WARNING SIGNS

It has been known for some decades that certain species of shark will, under certain circumstances, alter their body posture as a warning sign that they might launch a pre-emptive attack against an animal that they perceive to be a threat or a competitor. The Indo-Pacific grey reef shark was the first systematically investigated species. There are several features which combine to produce the classic so-called agonistic display: the lowering of the pectoral fins, the raising of the snout, the stiffening or even cessation of the swimming motion, the contortion of the body into an unnatural curve. As a shark will often lower its pectoral fins to increase its manoeuvrability, there is discussion as to whether this alone is a sufficient signal of agonistic intent. Nevertheless, any shark that appears to be swimming erratically should be neither followed nor photographed (the firing of an underwater flash gun has been known to trigger an attack by the photographed shark). Agonistic warning signs by sharks appear to be considerably more widespread than was

Sharks are magnificent and integral components of the ecosystems in which they occur. Divers who are fortunate enough to observe these animals underwater have a duty to champion their protection.

originally supposed. I recently saw a remarkable piece of video footage, filmed by a diver in the Bahamas who got in the water with a large tiger shark that was attempting to feed on a leatherback turtle. As the diver swam towards the tiger shark, it lowered its pectoral fins and began to swim in a slow, stiffened arc. When the woman ignored this, it turned, charged, and rammed her. Needless to say she got out of the water. It is not only of interest that this tiger shark displayed to her, but that it rammed, rather than bit her. This rather suggests that the tiger shark saw her as a competitor trying to help itself to the turtle the shark was assiduously hunting. Needless to say, butting / ramming seems to be a pretty serious warning sign by a shark. Gary Adkison, the dive manager of Walker's Cay, once was leading a group of divers along a reef when he observed a great hammerhead shark. He swam up to it and took a few photographs before it made off. He rejoined the dive group and a few minutes later the great hammerhead reappeared, swooped through the group of divers and rammed into Gary before disappearing!

ATTACKING TO FEED

The behaviour described above is either defensive or competitive in origin. Much more dangerous to humans, however, are attacks launched by sharks attempting to devour the victim. Such attacks are possible from sharks that are capable of biting chunks out of an animal too large to swallow whole. These sharks tend to be large, generalist feeders – feeding on a wide variety of prey items. Their teeth are serrated and more or less triangular in shape. The teeth of a shark that catches small fishes and swallows

them whole are usually thinner and more pointed, designed for impaling prey which is then gulped intact.

In our region, the three generalist predators most likely to be encountered in inshore waters are the bull shark, the tiger shark and the great hammerhead. All three species grow to considerable size, the latter two to about 6 metres. They are implicated in attacks on humans, and the bull and tiger shark are considered to be amongst the most dangerous of all sharks. Given their preference for warm, shallow water, they tend to come into contact with humans far more often than the potentially dangerous offshore sharks. The victims of such attacks tend to be surfers and swimmers – people who are mistaken for other creatures, or who, by splashing around, give off vibrations that the shark thinks indicate injury.

Sharks have the ability to signal threat warnings to other animals. This oceanic whitetip off Hawaii rapidly opened and shut its mouth and shook its head from side to side when I blocked its path and then swam towards it.

Offshore species of shark such as the oceanic whitetip, the silky shark *Carcharhinus falciformis,* and also, in all probability, other requiem sharks encountered in blue water, can aggressively investigate a human being. The oceanic whitetip is notorious for boldly approaching and bumping into a person in an apparent effort to determine if he or she is edible.

[opposite top] The bull shark is an immensely powerful generalist predator of inshore waters throughout this region.

[opposite bottom] The tiger shark *Galeocerdo cuvier* ranges from the shallowest to the deepest waters. In this region it tends to enter shallow water at night.

The oceanic whitetip shark will approach and often bump into a diver in open water. Other species of shark – including those more commonly seen on coral reefs – will also react to humans with considerably greater curiosity or even aggression in open water.

[opposite]
many sharks do most of
their feeding at dawn or
dusk (crepuscular) and
can be aggressive at
these times.

ATTACKS ON DIVERS

Thankfully, attacks on divers are extremely rare. A diver underwater is usually avoided or ignored. It goes without saying that whether diving or snorkelling with sharks, one should swim smoothly and not thrash about giving off erratic signals.

Many sharks are crepuscular in their feeding activities – they feed at dawn and dusk unless other opportunities arise. As such, they can become both more active and more aggressive towards humans at these times.

Strange as it may seem, it is not always the larger sharks that pose the greatest risk. Occasionally it is the youngsters that show a lack of respect, while the adults keep their distance. Some biologists think that these adults have attained their size through a prudent combination of fight or flight, while among the smaller sharks there is a sizeable proportion that will not reach adulthood precisely because of their excessive risk-taking.

SHARKS AND MARINE MAMMALS

Sharks often accompany marine mammals in open water, so swimming with them is rather more of a risk than is generally supposed. In various parts of the Indo-Pacific region I have seen silky, grey reef, oceanic whitetip, silvertip *Carcharhinus albimarginatus* and Galapagos sharks *C. galapagensis* swimming with, below or behind, a variety of marine mammals, including bottlenose dolphins *Tursiops truncatus*, false killer whales *Pseudorca crassidens* and pilot whales *Globicephala macrorhynchus*. These species of marine mammal exist in this region as do several of the species of shark mentioned above (as

well, of course, as very similar species). I have heard accounts of divers in the western Atlantic being molested or bumped into by large sharks when they entered the water to swim with marine mammals, so evidently the same state of affairs exists throughout the tropics. Sharks accompanying marine mammals can treat intruding humans with considerable aggression. It may be that the sharks mistake a snorkeller for an injured marine mammal and regard him or her as an easy meal; the excited echo-locating and swimming of marine mammals when divers/snorkellers swim with them can only increase the curiosity of any nearby or accompanying sharks. Not only will an occasional large shark, such as a tiger shark, stalk pods of the smaller marine mammals hoping for an easy meal, but there are also occasional reports of whole schools of sharks apparently hunting dolphins.

On more than one occasion when I have swum over to dolphins that were passing by a coral reef, the reef sharks reacted with alarming aggression towards me – presumably mistaking me for an injured dolphin.

FEEDING SHARKS

It has become commonplace for divers around the world to feed reef sharks in order to bring them in close enough to be properly observed and photographed. Indeed, given their natural shyness, this is the only reliable method of taking pictures of most of them. There are those who argue on a variety of grounds – respect for the animals, aesthetic, ecological impact, safety to divers – that shark feeding of any sort should be outlawed. It seems to me that when the positive aspects of shark feeding – interaction

with spectacular wildlife, education and the dispelling of myths, revenue to the local economy, a basis for conservation initiatives – are set against the negative, *responsible* shark feeding becomes acceptable. There are, however, elements of some types of shark feeding which are, to my mind, vulgar and sensationalistic. First and foremost is the hand-feeding of sharks. A chain-mail protected diver offers dead fish to the sharks by hand. While the hand (and, occasionally, other parts of the body) is inevitably bitten, the chain-mail offers protection. However, the shark, which cannot distinguish between where the dead fish ends and the human being begins, is, in effect, being conditioned to bite humans.

A simple improvement on the above method is for sharks to be offered dead fish on the end of a pole or hand-spear: this at least separates human from food item. It has been argued by behavioural ecologists that by offering sharks food in this way their hierarchical feeding processes, which are based on dominance and subservience, can be disrupted. The most sophisticated shark feeding method that I have seen was at Walker's Cay: the sharks feed from a frozen 'chumsicle' of fish parts that floats off the bottom. Once the chumsicle is in place there is no human interference with the feeding activities of the sharks – which ignore the divers.

THE SHARK TRUST SHARK FEEDING CODE

PRINCIPLE	RATIONALE
◗ NO INDISCRIMINATE SURFACE CHUMMING OR CHUMMING AROUND BOATS.	PREVENT ENTRAINMENT OF SHARKS TO VESSELS AND TO OTHER VESSEL-BASED ACTIVITIES.
◗ ONLY FEED SHARKS USING FREE–STANDING BAITS, OR BY POLE OR STICK, NOT BY HAND OR MOUTH.	ENSURE THAT SHARKS WILL NOT EXPECT FOOD DIRECTLY FROM DIVERS.
◗ MINIMIZE ALL HANDLING OF SHARKS, PARTICULARLY WHEN DONE AS A 'SHOW' FOR DIVERS.	RESPECT WILD ANIMALS! SHARKS SHOULD NOT BECOME USED TO BEING APPROACHED OR HANDLED BY DIVERS.
◗ DO NOT TAKE FISH FROM REEFS OR OTHER INSHORE HABITATS FOR FEEDS. USE FISH WASTE OR UNWANTED BY–CATCH.	MINIMIZE THE EFFECT OF REMOVING FISH FROM INSHORE POPULATIONS AND ECOSYSTEMS.
◗ BOATS SHOULD USE PERMANENT MOORINGS, NOT ANCHORS.	PREVENT ANCHOR DAMAGE TO SENSITIVE INSHORE HABITATS AND REEF ECOSYSTEMS.
◗ LOCATE FEEDING SITES IN CORAL RUBBLE OR SANDY AREAS.	ENSURE THAT DIVERS AND SHARKS DON'T DAMAGE LIVING REEFS.
◗ CONSIDER CAREFULLY THE RELATIVE LOCATIONS OF FEEDING SITES AND OTHER RECREATIONAL AREAS.	SEPARATE FEEDING SITES FROM POPULAR DIVING, SNORKELLING, SWIMMING AND FISHING AREAS.
◗ MINIMIZE THE NUMBER OF FEEDING SITES AND FEEDS, IF NECESSARY BY AGREEMENT WITH OPERATORS.	REDUCE OVERALL ECOLOGICAL AND BEHAVIOURAL IMPACTS OF SHARK FEEDING IN THE AREA.
◗ PROMOTE A STRONG DIVER EDUCATION PROGRAMME, COVERING THE LIFE HISTORY OF SHARKS, THEIR ECOLOGICAL ROLE, THE THREATS FROM MAN, DIVING CONDUCT.	ENSURE THAT ALL DIVERS ARE WELL TRAINED IN DIVING PROCEDURES AND THAT SHARK CONSERVATION AND AWARENESS ARE PROMOTED IN A SENSITIVE AND BALANCED MANNER.
◗ SEEK LEGAL PROTECTION FOR SHARKS AND THEIR HABITATS.	PROTECT HABITATS, DIVE SITES AND SHARK POPULATIONS EXPLOITED BY SHARK TOURISM.
◗ LIAISE WITH LOCAL FISHERMEN AND COMMUNITIES, SUPPORT CONSERVATION LOCALLY BY PROMOTING LOCAL EDUCATION AND INTERPRETATION PROGRAMMES.	SPREAD AWARENESS OF THE ECOLOGICAL AND ECONOMIC VALUE OF SHARKS AS WELL AS THEIR SPECIAL IMPORTANCE AS MARINE WILDLIFE AND THEIR SIGNIFICANCE TO LOCAL CULTURE.

[previous]
The Chumsicle Feed at Walker's Cay allows divers to observe and photograph many dozens of wild sharks.

SAFETY TIPS

It should be remembered that most sharks normally pose little threat to divers only because they are unfamiliar with them and their instincts warn them to treat anything unfamiliar with respect. If the large predatory sharks knew just how vulnerable a diver is, then things would be very different. All sharks are potentially dangerous and divers interacting with sharks should never become complacent. The following is a list garnered from my own experiences and the advice of others that should minimize, but cannot entirely eradicate, the risk of diving with sharks:

◉ Never swim erratically.

◉ Stay in a group.

◉ Avoid brightly coloured diving equipment when diving with sharks. White and yellow are particularly bad; the latter has been called 'yum-yum yellow' by biologists investigating the colour preferences of sharks. When attending a shark feed do not flail around; tuck your hands in to your side. A pale hand protruding from a dark wetsuit can look like a fish to a feeding shark: wear dark gloves. A dark dive hood is also recommended to conceal long or pale hair (especially blond, grey, white or silver hair) or a bald head.

◉ Avoid swimming with sharks at dawn and dusk.

◉ Be able to identify the species you see so as to make a preliminary estimate of the threat it is likely to pose.

◉ Be aware when swimming with marine mammals that if sharks are present they can be aggressive. If sharks do appear, do not thrash about but rather swim calmly and leave the water. Always wear mask, fins and snorkel and preferably a wetsuit when swimming with marine mammals. The mask will allow you to see any sharks. Fins and snorkel will allow you to swim calmly and efficiently. The wetsuit will offer protection should an investigating shark bump into you. Never free-swim with marine mammals where there is the possibility of encountering sharks.

▶ Leave shark feeding to experienced dive masters.

▶ Always carry a fluorescent orange safety flag or tube: if you are swept off a reef into deep water you may need to be collected quickly.

▶ Always swim back to the reef wall at the end of a dive and wait to be collected there.

▶ Never swim so far from a reef that you cannot quickly return to it. Do not allow yourself to be swept from a reef into open water. Sharks are geared to investigate an animal that leaves a reef and does not appear able to return.

▶ Never snorkel or dive in open water without a boat close at hand for rapid exit.

▶ Never attempt to follow or photograph a shark that appears to be swimming strangely.

▶ If, during a shark feed, the sharks seem particularly interested in your flash gun, turn it off: it is not unusual for feeding sharks to bump or bite underwater flash guns.

▶ Do not hesitate to abort a dive if the sharks are swimming rapidly or showing interest in you.

▶ If a large shark such as a tiger shark appears and then vanishes, keep a good look out for it as it may return.

▶ Spearfishing in the presence of sharks is asking for trouble: sharks react with extreme aggression in the presence of a struggling, wounded fish and will be rapidly attracted in from far away. This is unquestionably a dangerous activity in areas where there are sharks.

▶ Never allow the excitement of diving with sharks to cloud your common sense about when unacceptable risks are being taken. Think things through.

PART TWO

IDENTIFICATION

This section describes basic identification features that should allow a diver with a good view of a shark to identify it. The sharks listed here are the species a diver is more likely to encounter in our region. They are grouped according to the following distinctive features for a preliminary assessement.

Sharks with conspicuous fin markings

Sharks with conspicuous body markings

Sharks without conspicuous fin or body markings

The diagrams give accurate taxonomic information about the various species.

The small red sharks underneath a shark's name identify how dangerous this species is considered to be in a variety of contexts – to swimmers, surfers, spearfishermen and so on, rather than specifically to divers. The greater the number of small sharks, the higher the general threat – to a maximum of five.

BLACKTIP SHARK
Carcharhinus limbatus

IDENTIFICATION — There are small amounts of black on the extremities of various fins. The anal fin coloration is highly variable with black, dusky or pale colours all being possible. The body colour is normally fairly light and can range from almost white in silty, sandy areas, to platinum, pale bronze or grey. The snout, when viewed from the side, is fairly long and pointed. The back rises noticeably to the first dorsal fin.

DISTRIBUTION — Virtually worldwide in tropical and warm-temperate waters. Though it ranges offshore, it is more common in inshore waters. Common in this region.

SIZE — Attains over 2.5 metres, though most individuals are considerably smaller.

HABITAT — Likely to be seen in coral reef environments, over sand flats and in lagoon areas.

DIET — Feeds on a wide variety of bony fishes and on an occasional cephalopod or crustacean.

COMMENTS — This is a swift, active and agile shark. It is readily attracted into shark feeds by divers.

Carcharhinus limbatus

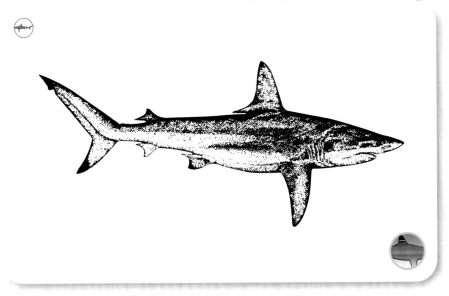

 # CARIBBEAN REEF SHARK
Carcharhinus perezi

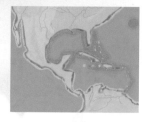

IDENTIFICATION	The dark coloration on the lower lobe of the tail is a useful clue to identification. Individuals can range in body shape from fairly slender to moderately heavy set. The snout is relatively short and bluntly rounded.
DISTRIBUTION	Bermuda, Florida, the Gulf of Mexico and Caribbean Sea; possibly off the east coast of Central and South America to Southern Brazil
SIZE	Attains about 3 metres, but more common in the 2 metre range.
HABITAT	A common shark of healthy coral reefs throughout this region. It will also venture offshore.
DIET	Eats a wide variety of bony fishes.
COMMENTS	A powerful and impressive predator that often attends shark feeds. During such feeds it normally ignores divers. The species is highly excitable when expecting to be fed or in the presence of speared fish. On rare occasions divers involved in shark feeding have been bitten.

Carcharhinus perezi

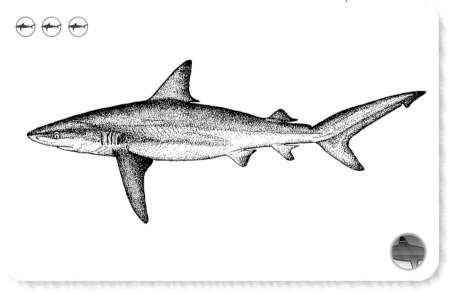

OCEANIC WHITETIP SHARK
Carcharhinus longimanus

IDENTIFICATION   This shark is easily identified by the combination of the first dorsal fin's coloration and shape: the apex has a splotchy white marking and the fin is large and rounded. The other fins have varying degrees of splotchy white markings; the anal fin can have dark marks while juveniles also have dark markings on this and other fin extremities. The pectoral fins are large and rounded. The upper body can be light brown to bronze and this yields, via a splotchy interface, to the pale underside. The species is often accompanied by pilotfishes.

DISTRIBUTION   An oceanic shark of tropical to warm-temperate waters worldwide.

SIZE   Attains over 3 metres.

HABITAT   This is a truly oceanic shark whose numbers increase further from land. It favours the surface layers of the ocean. The oceanic whitetip often accompanies or is in the environ of marine mammals. It will also hang off deep-water reefs and occasionally venture inshore.

DIET   It feeds on a wide variety of oceanic prey items from bony fishes to cephalopods. The white fin markings may act as a lure to attract fishes, as a species recognition signal, or both.

COMMENTS   An inquisitive, bold and dangerous shark that will readily approach an open-water object such as a floating boat or diver. It will circle and bump any potential food source with its snout.

Carcharhinus longimanus

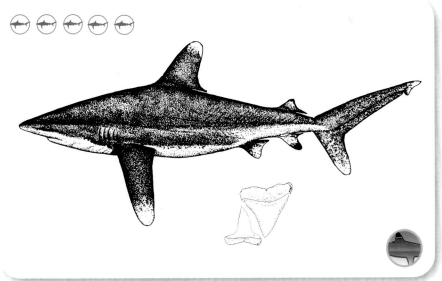

TIGER SHARK
Galeocerdo cuvier

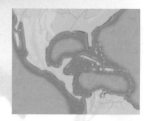

IDENTIFICATION Juveniles are covered on their sides and back with a series of dark spots and dashes on a tan background. These change into vertical dark stripes on larger individuals, hence the common name. In individuals over about 4 metres, the stripes tend to fade. The head is massive and blunt-snouted, the mouth enormous and the eyes very large and dark. The first dorsal fin is broad-based and the body tends to become noticeably more slender behind it. Tiger sharks, especially mature females, can be extremely bulky.

DISTRIBUTION Global distribution in tropical and temperate seas, though not recorded from the Mediterranean.

SIZE Probably to about 6 metres.

HABITAT A roaming shark that can occur from shallow inshore waters to deep offshore waters. The tendency of the tiger shark to stay down at depth during the day makes it appear considerably more scarce than it actually is. A marlin struggling on the end of a game-fisherman's line will often draw large tiger sharks up from the depths.

DIET Possibly the most wide-ranging diet of any shark species: bony fishes, sharks, rays, crustaceans, cephalopods, sea birds, turtles, sea snakes, garbage.

COMMENTS Though implicated in numerous attacks on surfers, the tiger shark normally ignores divers. It does occasionally follow dive boats that leave one area because of its presence only to reappear at the new location!

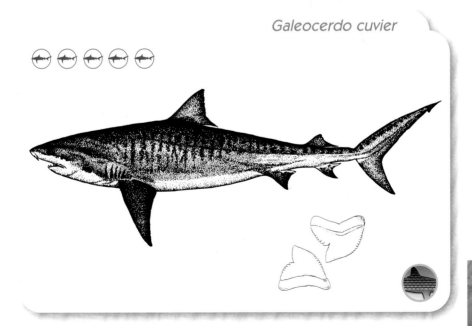

Galeocerdo cuvier

WHALE SHARK
Rhincodon typus

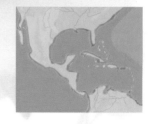

IDENTIFICATION A large to gigantic shark covered in white spots and both vertical and horizontal stripes.

DISTRIBUTION Occurs in warm waters worldwide, but absent from the Mediterranean.

SIZE Maximum size probably about 12 metres, though there are occasional reports of considerably larger individuals.

HABITAT May be encountered from shallow to deep water.

DIET Feeds mainly on animal plankton (zooplankton), although it does also eat small bony fishes.

COMMENTS This gentle giant can be curious and can approach a diver for a close look provided he or she is swimming calmly. Some divers cannot resist grabbing hold of a fin and hitching a ride – an unfortunate action as the shark will probably then dive and not return.

Rhincodon typus

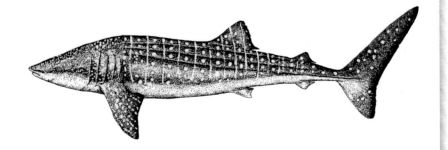

BLACKNOSE SHARK
Carcharhinus acronotus

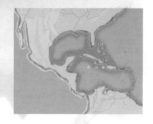

IDENTIFICATION	A small to medium-sized requiem shark with a light body coloration. There is a noticeable dusky mark on the end of the snout.
DISTRIBUTION	North Carolina, the Bahamas, Gulf of Mexico and Caribbean, the Atlantic coast of South America to southern Brazil.
SIZE	Most individuals are less than 1.5 metres in length.
HABITAT	An inshore shark of sea-grass beds, sand flats and coral rubble areas.
DIET	Small bony fishes.
COMMENTS	A timid shark that is hunted by larger sharks in shallow water. The blacknose shark has been observed in captivity to perform a threat display – back arched, snout elevated, pectoral fins lowered.

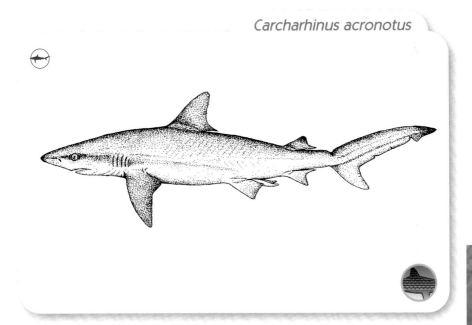

Carcharhinus acronotus

NURSE SHARK
Ginglymostoma cirratum

IDENTIFICATION

The nurse shark has a very large second dorsal fin, a first dorsal fin located far back – above the pelvic fins, and very small eyes. The caudal fin is relatively long and paddle-shaped. Because of the proximity of the fourth and fifth gill slit, the nurse shark looks as if it only has four gill slits. There are pronounced nasal barbels.

DISTRIBUTION

Found in shallow water on both sides of the Americas: in the eastern Pacific from Baja California to Peru, in the western Atlantic from Rhode Island south to Bermuda, the eastern seaboard of the United States, the Gulf of Mexico, Caribbean and the Atlantic coast of South America to southern Brasil. It also occurs off the tropical western African coast and occasionally further north and south.

SIZE

Maximum about 3 metres.

HABITAT

Occurs in a wide variety of shallow-water habitats including coral reefs, rubble areas, sand flats and mangrove creeks. Being nocturnal, the nurse shark is often seen lying on the bottom during the day.

DIET

Feeds on a wide variety of bottom-dwelling invertebrates, such as crabs, shrimps, spiny lobsters, octopuses, as well as bony fishes, which it presumably sucks into its mouth when they are at rest.

COMMENTS

One of the most commonly seen sharks in our region and usually docile if unmolested. It can be pugnacious in the presence of food.

Ginglymostoma cirratum

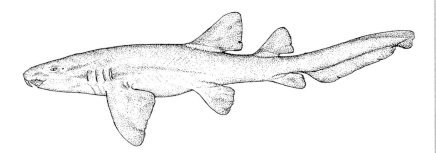

BULL SHARK
Carcharhinus leucas

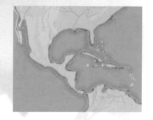

IDENTIFICATION   The bull shark is heavily to massively built, with a short and bluntly rounded snout, small yellowish eyes, a broad-based first dorsal fin and no conspicuous fin or body markings.

DISTRIBUTION   A worldwide shark of inshore tropical and subtropical continental waters (though absent from the Red sea); it also occurs off some island groups, such as Fiji and the Philippines, and penetrates certain rivers.

SIZE   To about 3.5 metres.

HABITAT   The bull shark can be seen on coral reefs, though it is more at home in turbid inshore waters such as estuaries, lagoons and sand flats. It readily enters rivers and penetrates far upstream. In our region the bull shark is recorded from numerous rivers, including the Mississippi and the Amazon, as well as from Lake Nicaragua.

DIET   The bull shark has an extremely wide range of food items – sharks, rays, bony fishes, shellfish, cephalopods, sea turtles, sea birds, marine mammals (dolphins), terrestrial mammals (dogs, rats).

COMMENTS   The formidable size, large mouth, large serrated teeth, broad diet and tendency of the bull shark to occur in murky inshore, brackish or fresh water where human beings are likely to be encountered fishing or swimming, explain the very high attribution of attacks on humans to this species. In other conditions – clearer water or reef environments where humans are scuba diving rather than splashing around on the surface – the danger posed by this species is considerably reduced.

Carcharhinus leucas

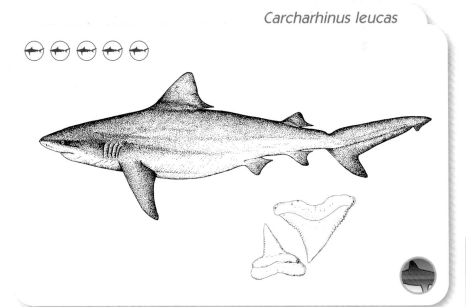

SILKY SHARK
Carcharhinus falciformis

IDENTIFICATION   The body, except in pregnant females, is fairly thin when viewed from the side and the snout markedly pointed. The eye is fairly small. The first dorsal fin is relatively low, the apex being more rounded than pointed. The rear edge of the first dorsal fin can originate behind the apex, making the fin appear to slant backwards. The first dorsal fin is placed fairly far back: an imaginary line drawn straight down from its forward origin will meet the belly well behind the rear inner corner of the pectoral fin. The second dorsal fin is relatively low with a very long free rear tip.

DISTRIBUTION   Occurs in tropical and subtropical waters worldwide.

SIZE   Attains over 3 metres in length.

HABITAT   An open-water shark that normally occurs within reasonable distance of land (a situation converse to that of the oceanic whitetip). It can also be seen hanging off deep-water reefs and also accompanies marine mammals.

DIET   A swift and agile predator that eats mainly bony fishes.

COMMENTS   A bold and occasionally dangerous shark. When feeding on bait fishes, highly excited silkies have been known to harass and even bite observing divers. The silky can also aggressively investigate divers on night dives. I have been chased up on to the top of a Red Sea reef by two silkies at dusk.

Carcharhinus falciformis

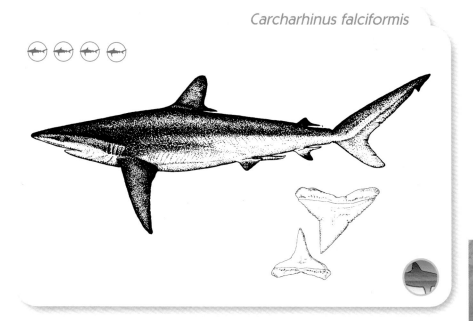

GALAPAGOS SHARK
Carcharhinus galapagensis

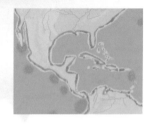

IDENTIFICATION The Galapagos shark is a large requiem shark which is very similar in appearance to the Caribbean reef shark. Though it lacks pronounced fin markings, the lower lobe of the caudal fin can have a dusky coloration. The Galapagos shark can be tentatively distinguished from the Caribbean reef shark underwater by the longer and slightly more pointed snout of the Galapagos shark, and also by the first dorsal fin. In the Galapagos shark this is usually moderately high and pointed and with a vertical rear edge; the first dorsal fin of the Caribbean reef shark is more variable.

DISTRIBUTION Worldwide, but usually associated with oceanic islands. In the Atlantic this includes Bermuda, Cape Verde and Ascension. In our region it is recorded from the Virgin Islands.

SIZE Attains over 3 metres, possibly nearly 4 metres.

HABITAT Usually in the vicinity of oceanic islands where it ranges from shallow to deep water.

DIET A variety of benthic (bottom-dwelling) and free-swimming bony fishes and cephalopods.

COMMENTS A large, fast, powerful and potentially dangerous shark. Off continental coastlines (including our region) it tends to be replaced by the very similar dusky shark *Carcharhinus obscurus* which has slightly lower dorsal fins. I have not seen underwater photographs of the dusky.

Carcharhinus galapagensis

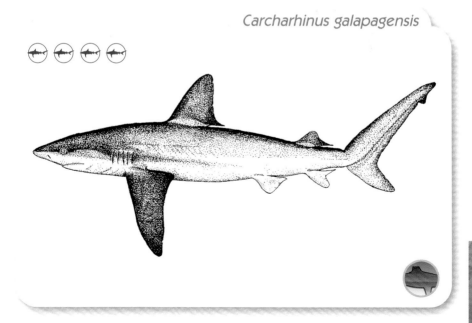

SANDBAR SHARK
Carcharhinus plumbeus

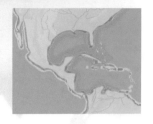

IDENTIFICATION The sandbar shark can be identified by the enormous first dorsal fin.

DISTRIBUTION Widespread in tropical and temperate waters.

SIZE To about 3 metres.

HABITAT The sandbar shark occurs in shallow, murky, inshore environments, including river mouths. It also cruises along the edge of the continental shelf to depths of several hundred metres.

DIET The sandbar shark specializes in feeding on a wide variety of small bony fishes.

COMMENTS It avoids coral reef environments and so is rarely seen by divers. Furthermore it is not, unlike many other members of the genus, attracted to dead fish and so does not appear at shark feeds.

David Fleetham, Innerspace Visions.

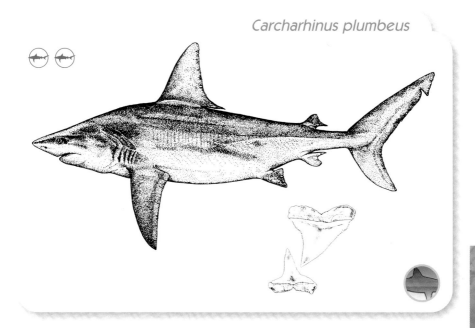

Carcharhinus plumbeus

LEMON SHARK
Negaprion brevirostris

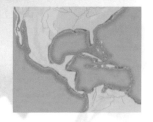

IDENTIFICATION The lemon shark has a very large second dorsal fin. Unlike the nurse shark (see page 70), the first dorsal fin is located between the pectoral and pelvic fins. The sand tiger shark *Carcharias taurus* has similarly sized and positioned dorsal fins (see page 82 for distinguishing details). The lemon shark's body can vary in colour from pale yellow to dark grey (depending on substrate). The eyes are small, the snout short and bluntly rounded. In males the body can be fairly thin, while females can be somewhat bulky.

DISTRIBUTION In the eastern Pacific from both sides of the Baja Peninsula to Ecuador. In the western Atlantic from New Jersey to southern Brazil. Also sporadically present along the tropical African coast of the eastern Atlantic.

SIZE Attains about 3.5 metres.

HABITAT The lemon shark prefers inshore waters and favours creeks, mangrove channels, sand and mud flats and river mouths. It can enter fresh water but to a lesser extent than the bull shark.

DIET Mainly bony fishes but also rays and crayfish.

COMMENTS The lemon shark is readily attracted by fish bait. Scientists who observed lemon sharks competing with other sharks for offered bait have commented on this being an unusually cunning shark adept at sneaking in on the food source.

Negaprion brevirostris

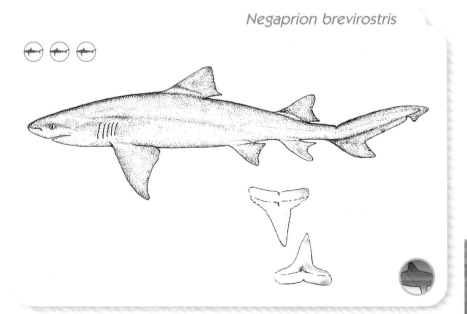

SAND TIGER SHARK
Carcharias taurus

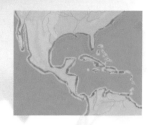

IDENTIFICATION Its two large dorsal fins and their placement make this species superficially similar to the lemon shark (page 80). Unlike the lemon shark, the sand tiger is often seen hovering just off the bottom. The snout of the sand tiger is more pointed than that of the lemon shark and the large teeth bristle noticeably from the mouth. The body can be marked with dull spots.

DISTRIBUTION Irregularly distributed in temperate and tropical waters worldwide. In the northwestern Atlantic it occurs from the Gulf of Maine south to Florida and the northern Gulf of Mexico. It is also recorded from Bermuda and the Bahamas. In Australia it is called the grey nurse shark, in South Africa it is called the ragged-tooth shark.

SIZE Probably reaches over 3 metres.

HABITAT From shallow to fairly deep water. The sand tiger shark is occasionally seen by divers hovering in small groups in the immediate vicinity of wrecks.

DIET This shark feeds, often in co-ordinated groups, on a wide variety of bony fishes. It also eats small sharks and rays, cephalopods and crustaceans.

COMMENTS This is a relatively inoffensive shark whose ferocious appearance has led to its being blamed for attacks it has not committed. This species' tendency to form aggregations off deep-water wrecks has facilitated overfishing by sports fishermen.

Doug Perrine, Innerspace Visions

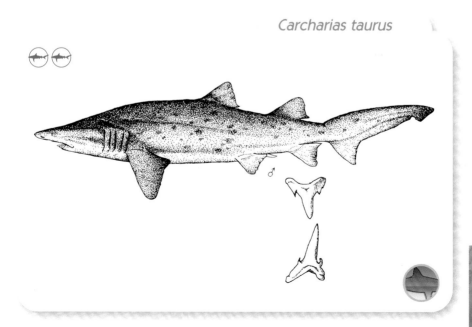

Carcharias taurus

CARIBBEAN SHARPNOSE SHARK
Rhizoprionodon porosus

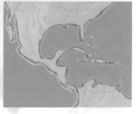

IDENTIFICATION   A small, pale grey shark with relatively large eyes and a fairly sharply rounded snout. Immediately in front of the anal fin are a pair of ridges (just visible in the identifying photograph).

DISTRIBUTION   Bahamas, Caribbean, Atlantic coast of South America to Uruguay.

SIZE   Attains just over 1 metre.

HABITAT   A common shark of shallow environments such as sand flats, sea-grass beds, lagoons and tidal creeks.

DIET   Small bony fishes, small cephalopods and molluscs.

COMMENTS   The Caribbean sharpnose shark is visually inseparable from the Atlantic sharpnose shark *R. terraenovae* which occurs in the Gulf of Mexico, around Florida and north to New Brunswick. In the Gulf of Mexico the Atlantic sharpnose shark enters shallow water in spring and retreats to deeper water in the autumn. It is not certain that these two sharks are indeed separate species.

Rhizoprionodon porosus

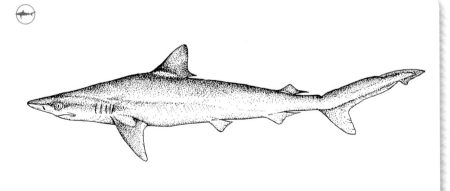

BONNETHEAD
Sphyrna tiburo

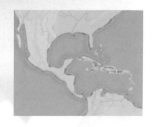

IDENTIFICATION	A small hammerhead shark with a distinctive shovel-shaped head.
DISTRIBUTION	In the eastern Pacific from southern California to Ecuador. In the western Atlantic from North Carolina (and occasionally further north), the Bahamas, Cuba, the continental coastlines of the Gulf of Mexico and Caribbean. Recorded in South America south to Brazil.
SIZE	To 1.5 metres.
HABITAT	Typically encountered in inshore waters – in lagoons, over sand flats and sea-grass beds, coral reef areas and in estuaries.
DIET	Mostly crustaceans.
COMMENTS	An active, shallow-water hammerhead. Studies on a population in an enclosure in Florida revealed complex behavioural patterns related both to hunting and to social interactions between individuals.

Doug Perrine, Innerspace Visions

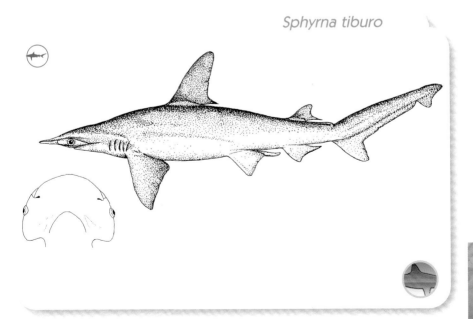

Sphyrna tiburo

SCALLOPED HAMMERHEAD
Sphyrna lewini

IDENTIFICATION A medium to large bronze-coloured hammerhead (that looks grey at depth). The forward edge of the hammer has five pronounced indentations. The first dorsal fin is quite high, the second dorsal, pelvic and anal fins are relatively small.

DISTRIBUTION Occurs in tropical and warm-temperate waters worldwide with the possible exception of the Mediterranean.

SIZE Probably reaches about 4 metres, though more common in the 2 to 3 metre range.

HABITAT Occurs from shallow inshore to oceanic waters.

DIET Bony fishes, small sharks and rays. Scalloped hammerheads encountered in relatively deep water off the edges of reefs during the day probably move into shallow, sandy areas at night to hunt fishes buried in the sand.

COMMENTS The hammerhead most commonly encountered by divers in many parts of the world. In the Indo-Pacific it often forms schools of many dozens, or even hundreds of individuals. There are occasional, tantalizing reports of equivalent sightings in the western Atlantic – from the oil rigs off the Texan coast of the Gulf of Mexico, as well as off San Salvador. The tendency of the scalloped hammerhead to prefer cooler water means that it may tend to school beyond the depths of recreational divers in this region.

Sphyrna lewini

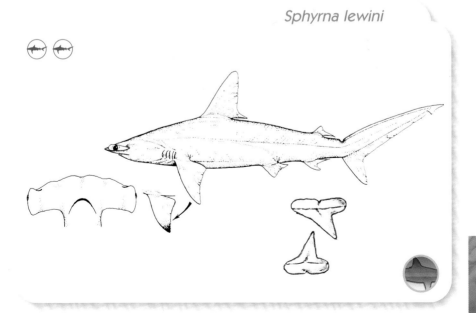

GREAT HAMMERHEAD
Sphyrna mokarran

IDENTIFICATION	A large to colossal hammerhead. The head and fin shapes are quite different from those of the scalloped hammerhead. The first dorsal fin is enormous and sickle-shaped. The second dorsal, anal and pelvic fins are all quite large; the pelvic fins have a pronounced concave curve to their rear edge. The head is rectangular with one noticeable central indentation and lesser depressions at the nostrils. The body is grey.
DISTRIBUTION	Pan-oceanic in tropical and warm-temperate waters. More common off continental coasts. Rare in the Mediterranean.
SIZE	Perhaps in excess of 6 metres.
HABITAT	From shallow inshore waters to the open sea.
DIET	Feeds on a wide variety of bony fishes and also small sharks. It also has a marked fondness for stingrays: one has been observed immobilizing a stingray by first biting off its pectoral wing tips. A great hammerhead can often have numerous stingray barbs embedded in its head.
COMMENTS	An uncommon but magnificent and powerful predator. Doubtless the most dangerous of hammerheads, this species will approach divers closely. There are occasional reports of great hammerheads rushing towards a diver when he first jumps into blue water for a deep dive.

Sphyrna mokarran

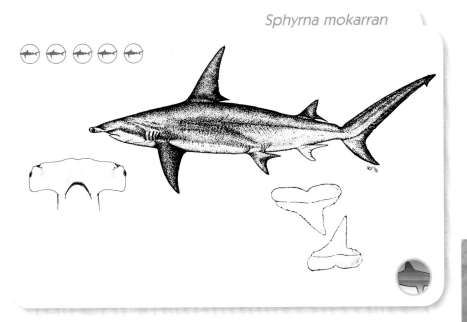

THE SHARK TRUST

Established in 1997, the Shark Trust promotes the study, management and conservation of sharks, skates and rays.

The Shark Trust is calling for:
- sustainably managed shark fisheries
- reduced shark bycatch in other fisheries
- legal protection for threatened species
- conservation of breeding and nursery habitats
- increased research into shark biology and ecology
- development of national and international management and conservation strategies
- international conservation and research initiatives, including tag and release programmes
- increased public awareness of the conservation needs of these vulnerable animals

Please help to Save our Sharks!
Join now to receive your supporter pack, free shark poster and regular newsletters.

Adopt a shark, and support your choice of research and conservation projects around the world.

The Shark Trust
c/o The National Marine Aquarium,
Rope Walk,
Coxside,
Plymouth PL4 OLF,
U.K.
Tel: 01752-672008.
Website: www.sharktrust.org.
Email: sharktrust@national-aquarium.co.uk.
Registered Charity No. 1064185.

SHARK TRUST

Date	Location	Depth	Sharks Observed

Date	Location	Depth	Sharks Observed